First in the Field

Baseball Hero Jackie Robinson

To my mother, Mattie, who gave me the love and

encouragement to pursue my dreams.

And to my siblings, Butch, Velda, and Kevin,

who continue to lend support and an ear.

For the Negro leaguers, who blazed the trail in baseball as well as life. Milestone

Media, Inc. pledges to give a portion of the royalties from this book to the Negro

leagues pension fund. We thank you for your sacrifice and contribution.

Text © 1998 by Milestone Media, Inc.

Printed in the United States of America.

First Edition
1 3 5 7 9 10 8 6 4 2

This book is set in 12-point Gill Sans.
Designed by Stephanie Bart-Horvath.

Library of Congress Cataloging-in-Publication Data
Dingle, Derek T.
First in the field : baseball hero Jackie Robinson / Derek T. Dingle.
p.   cm.
Summary: a biography which discusses the discrimination faced by Jackie Robinson, the baseball legend who
became the first African-American to play major league baseball.
ISBN 0-7868-0348-7 (trade)-ISBN 0-7868-2289-9 (lib. bdg.)
1. Robinson, Jackie, 1919-1972-Juvenile literature. 2. Baseball players-United States-Biography-Juvenile literature. 3.
Afro-American baseball players-United States-Biography-Juvenile literature. 4. Discrimination in sports-United
States-History-20th century-Juvenile literature. [1. Robinson, Jackie, 1919-1972. 2. Afro-American baseball players.
3. Baseball players. 4. Afro-Americans-Biography.] I. Title. GV865.R6D56 1998 796.357'092-dc21
[B]   97-41333

First in the Field

Baseball Hero Jackie Robinson

Derek T. Dingle

Hyperion Books for Children

NEW YORK

FIRST CRACK AT BAT

When I was growing up, I knew Jackie Robinson and Joe Louis and Sugar Ray Robinson and what they meant. I realize the only reason I made it was because of a man like Jackie Robinson. I would like the next generation to understand a man who stood so tall.

—Hank Aaron

UP FROM POVERTY

When Jackie Robinson first cracked his bat into major-league baseball in 1947, most of today's greats weren't even born. Few families owned a TV set—and if they did it was black and white. But no home was without a radio. Families would gather around it or flock to Ebbets Field in Brooklyn to cheer the Dodgers on and to see Jackie Robinson—the first African-American ever to play in the major leagues.

Boy, could he play. Jackie could hit the ball hard, field the best, run the fastest, and, best of all, steal the most bases. Some say he could steal three bases on one pitch. Jackie was a legend.

But Jackie was not always a star. When he was a kid, he spent most of his time day-dreaming about being a baseball player. Like most boys his age, he talked about playing in the big leagues. Like all African-American boys, he knew he could only play in the Negro leagues, teams of first-rate players that endured third-rate conditions.

As a seven-year-old, Jackie began his baseball career doing what he would do again and again—fighting for his right to play. That first time, he fought to play in his own neighborhood. He wanted to show his skills to the older boys on the block, but they were in no hurry to pick him for their teams. Still, every day after school, Jackie would tag along with his brother Mack and his friends. Mack was older than Jackie and the best athlete in the neighborhood.

Even as a child, Jackie seemed ready to
in the world.

When Mack played baseball with his friends, Jackie sat on the sidelines, watching how Mack tore into the ball time after time. As Mack rounded the bases, it seemed to Jackie as if his brother were gliding on air. To Jackie, Mack was a hero. He was the fastest, the strongest, and the coolest. Jackie wanted to be just like him.

After school Jackie followed Mack and his friends to the sandlot. There they used rocks for bases and sawed-off broomsticks for bats. One afternoon, they were short one player.

"We need another player if we are going to play," said the captain of one of the teams.

Jackie sat on the sidelines fidgeting. He wanted to play so badly. But none of the older boys looked his way. Finally Mack, the other team captain, looked around the sandlot. "What about my brother?" he said. "He's real good at dodgeball."

"Dodgeball isn't baseball," the other captain said.

The debate went on until, in the interest of getting the game started, the boys decided to let young Jackie play. But they put him way out in left field, away from the action, and they would not let him bat when it was his turn.

Behind by two runs, the team finally let Jackie bat. On the first pitch, he swung too quickly and missed the ball. All the boys on both sides laughed, except for Mack. On the second pitch, Jackie swung with all his might, smacking the ball between first and second bases. With a burst of speed, he rounded first base to second before the players could throw the ball back to the pitcher's mound.

Jackie stood at second base. Should he wait for the next player to hit the ball and advance to third? Or should he take matters into his own hands? He nervously eyed third base. As the pitcher threw the ball to the next batter, Jackie stole third, even though the batter did not connect with the ball. All the players—including Mack—were startled by Jackie's lightning speed and boldness.

The pitcher threw another pitch to the batter, who hit a grounder. Jackie dashed toward home plate. The pitcher scooped up the grounder, whipped around, and threw it to the catcher at home plate to stop Jackie in his tracks. Jackie slid into home as the ball touched the catcher's mitt. But all that Mack and the other guys on the field could see was a cloud of dust at home plate. When the scene cleared, the players realized that Jackie was safely at home while the catcher scrambled to find the ball.

Everyone cheered. But no one was prouder than Mack, who smiled broadly and patted his dusty brother on the back.

"Where did you learn to play like that?" the other team captain asked as he approached them.

Jackie brushed his stained clothes and quipped, "Dodgeball."

From that day on, he played with the big boys. It was not, however, the last time that Jackie Robinson would have to prove himself on a baseball field.

A rare portrait of the Robinson clan (left to right): Mack, Jackie, Mallie (seated), Edgar, Willa Mae, and Frank.

FOULING OUT

Jackie Robinson was born in 1919 on the same plantation that his grandparents were forced to work as slaves before President Abraham Lincoln signed the Emancipation Proclamation in 1863. Although Jackie's parents were not in physical bondage, Mallie and Jerry Robinson—married since 1909—endured the hardship of being tenant farmers, toiling in the fields for a meager twelve dollars a month.

They were already having trouble making ends meet when Jackie was born. In addition to this new member of the family, they had to feed three growing young boys—Edgar, eleven; Frank, nine; Mack, seven—and one girl, five-year-old Willa Mae. But Mallie was determined to make life better for her clan, encouraging Jerry to negotiate with the plantation owner about making him a "half-cropper" so that instead of working for a pittance, he would receive half the profits from the crops produced. Even with the extra money, Jerry could not take the oppressive life of being a farmer, and he left Cairo, Georgia, to see what else the world had to offer, abandoning his thirty-year-old wife and five children.

After Jerry left, the plantation owner ordered Mallie off his property. Mallie sold what little she had and, carrying tattered suitcases, took her family on a long, exhausting train ride to California, where she believed that she could create a new life for her family with the help of her brother Burton. Jackie was only six months old when the Robinsons arrived at their new home.

Mallie worked hard, taking two jobs as a domestic. Even though she would get up before daylight to go to work and come home exhausted, she still spent time with the Robinson kids, preaching to them the importance of family unity, religion, education, and kindness to others. Her example demonstrated hard work and perseverance—two qualities that would stick with Jackie the rest of his life. Within seven years, she saved enough to move to 1212 Pepper Street in Pasadena, California. Because of the size of the modest, two-story home, the Robinson kids called it "The Castle."

> Mallie's example demonstrated hard work and perseverance—two qualities that would stick with Jackie the rest of his life.

African-Americans were subjected to Jim Crow laws after the Civil War, primarily in the South. For more than eighty years, blacks could not drink at the same water cooler, sit at the same lunch counter, or use the same public accommodations.

Times were still rough for the Robinson family at The Castle. Young Jackie and his family were the only African-Americans living on the tree-lined block. They still did not have much money. Jackie often went to school hungry.

Young Jackie grew into a skilled player and a fierce competitor in every sport he played. He was so talented that his grade-school classmates would often bribe him to play on their team by offering part of their lunches or even a dollar. Jackie would take the money home and give it to his family.

He found a bit of consolation in sports. Even though he was applauded for his athletic skills, Jackie sometimes felt like an outsider. He was often teased and called names because of the color of his skin. He would ask himself, if everyone liked what he did on the playground so much, why did they treat him so badly?

Jackie sought solace at the movies, where he saw his other role model—besides his older brother Mack, by now a lightning-quick high-school track star—boxing legend Joe Louis.

The wiry, energetic Jackie and his pal "Little Jack" Gordon went to the local movie theater to see the big, brawny boxer, who was known as the "Brown Bomber"

One of Jackie's childhood heroes, heavyweight boxing champion Joe Louis—better known as the "Brown Bomber"—demonstrated that blacks could compete with whites on equal terms.

for his coffee-colored complexion and his explosive right hook. Because Jackie and Little Jack were black, they had to sit in a special section of the theater. Jackie forgot about that, though, sitting in the dark theater and watching the black-and-white image of Joe Louis clobbering yet another opponent in the ring. Jackie would swing his hands furiously, imitating the champ's every move. The two friends' viewing was often cut short when the usher would shoo them out of the theater for making too much of a racket. As Jackie made his way home, he would marvel at the rare sight of a black man competing as an equal with a white man and emerging a winner.

Despite the example of the Brown Bomber and the teachings of his mother, Jackie was frustrated by the twin demons of poverty and racism. Before the Civil Rights movement in the 1950s and 1960s, black people and other nonwhites often experienced segregation in more than theaters and restaurants. They could only play in the neighborhood YMCA one day a week and were only occasionally allowed to take a dip in the city's huge public swimming pool. Jackie sought out others who could relate to his experience. Unfortunately, Jackie fell in with the wrong crowd. He joined the Pepper Street Gang, a multicultural group of rebels who would stir up trouble throughout the neighborhood. The members of the rowdy gang were black, Mexican, and Japanese kids who lived a few blocks away from The Castle and, like Jackie, were treated as outcasts.

It was in the Pasadena of the late 1920s that Jackie suffered one of his greatest humiliations. Once Jackie and his friends were escorted to jail at gunpoint by the sheriff because they went for a swim in the local reservoir. Detained and interrogated under hot lights for hours by the sheriff and his deputies, Jackie and his friends suffered from heat exhaustion. They begged for something cold to drink or eat. The deputies brought Jackie and his friends watermelon and placed it on the floor. Eating off the floor, they consumed the watermelon to nourish their dehydrated bodies. The officers jeered and photographed the youths as they gulped down the fruit. It was a day that Jackie would not forget, a memory that fueled his bitterness—and determination to elevate his status.

Jackie became leader of the pack. His gang was different than those of today. They did not carry knives or guns, but they did engage in all sorts of mischief. The gang would stop traffic by throwing rocks at cars and streetlights, or take revenge on a homeowner who called them names by putting thick, sticky tar on his lawn. Jackie's mother found out about the tar incident and confronted her youngest child. With his head bowed in shame, Jackie led his band of marauders back to the gooey patch to clean it up.

But Mallie Robinson's scolding did not stop his activities with the Pepper Street Gang. Jackie's salvation came through the church.

One bright Sunday morning, the Robinsons went to their house of worship, Scotts Methodist Church, to meet the new minister. As usual, Jackie was restless, shifting around on the wooden bench in the pews. He would much rather be outside playing ball or causing mis-

chief than listening to another boring sermon. But the tall, redheaded Pastor Karl Downs was different. He was a young, energetic, and athletic minister who played basketball and softball. One day, Pastor Downs sought out the leader of the Pepper Street Gang at their favorite street corner. Pastor Downs told Jackie and the boys that he was organizing clubs and sports teams. He convinced the rowdies to give the church program a try. Jackie was so taken by the young minister that eventually he volunteered to be a Sunday school teacher in Downs's church.

Pastor Downs convinced the impressionable young Jackie to put his energy once again into sports. Now he could improve his athletic skills in a place where he would not be an outsider, in an organized church league. It did not take Jackie long to trade his gang membership for a team uniform.

> Jackie became leader of the pack. His gang was different than those of today. They did not carry knives or guns. . . .

SCHOOL DAYS

While the teachings of Pastor Downs helped turn him around, it was the athletic feats of his older brother Mack that inspired him. Jackie's muscular older brother excelled at basketball, baseball, and track and field, setting records in junior high school, high school, and college.

Mack was so good that he was picked to compete at the 1936 Olympics in Berlin, Germany. The bleary-eyed Robinson clan woke at 2 A.M. to hear the Olympics being broadcast from Germany. They huddled around the radio as the announcer called the finals of the 200-meter dash. All of the Robinsons cheered Mack as the young sprinter blasted from the starting blocks. "First out of the blocks is Mack Robinson. He is just flying. But here

comes Jesse Owens. It's Robinson and Owens down to the wire. And it's Owens crossing the finish line."

The Robinson family fell silent. Jesse Owens would take Mack's place in history. Even so, Mallie said in hushed tones, "I am proud of my boy."

Jackie decided then and there that he would never finish second—in anything, or to anyone, including his brother Mack. In high school, he earned letters in basketball, football, track, and baseball. In basketball, he led his team in rebounding and scoring. He played running back

Another one of Jackie's idols was his brother, Mack, a track-and-field star. He set records at Pasadena Junior College in such events as the broad jump (right) and competed in the 1936 Olympic Games, where he won the silver medal in the 200-meter dash (Mack is shown at the Olympic trials, above right). The legendary Jesse Owens captured the gold.

and quarterback on the football field. In track-and-field events, he ran against—and beat—his older brother's records. But on the baseball field, he demonstrated his greatest skills: power hitting and stealing bases.

After high school, Jackie was ready to tackle his brother's records at Mack's alma mater—Pasadena Junior College. While attending college, Jackie finally shook the long shadow that his brother cast.

One warm spring day, Jackie competed in two different events in two different cities. In the morning, Jackie traveled to Claremont, California, for a track-and-field event with his friend Johnny Burke. Less than a half hour away, the tire on their car blew out.

"I can't believe it. We're never going to make the meet," said Jackie. He was worried that if he showed up late, he wouldn't be allowed to compete.

"What's wrong, boys?" said the driver of a passing car. Jackie was in luck. It was the dean of his college. The dean offered his spare tire, which fortunately fit. Jackie and his friend left behind a trail of dust as they sped to the track meet. Jackie arrived just as his event—the broad jump competition—began, but he had no time to warm up. On his last of three attempts the lean, muscular athlete jumped 25 feet, 6½ inches, setting a new junior college national record for the broad jump—the record formerly held by Mack.

Jackie could not believe that he had broken his idol's record. But he had no time to pat himself on the back. He made a mad dash to a waiting car and headed to Glendale, California, for the state junior college baseball championship. Arriving mid-game, Jackie belted two hits and stole a base, helping his team win the championship. He was named the Most Valuable Junior College Player in Southern California in 1938.

Whenever Jackie made a special achievement in sports, he was always inspired by Mack's example. Unfortunately, he was always reminded that he had to rise above racism. Even though Mack was a great athlete with an Olympic medal, the only job that he could get was that of a street sweeper.

Despite the depressing reality, the spirit of the strapping young college star was boosted whenever he heard the cries "Go, Jackie, Go" from his own personal cheering section—his brother Frank. Although Jackie idolized Mack, he felt closest to Frank. Frank would often tell him, "Whatever happens, I'll be there for you, little brother."

One night in 1938, Jackie was at a neighbor's house playing cards when the phone rang. Frank, he learned, had been in a motorcycle accident. At the hospital, he

could see the pain that was etched on Frank's face. His mother was crying. Jackie grieved for his brother that night, and the next morning, Frank died. Jackie would never forget Frank and would dedicate himself to excelling in sports as a way of honoring his dead brother.

That's just what Jackie did when he attended UCLA for two years, becoming the university's first "four-letter" man, establishing records in football, baseball, track, and basketball! Because of his athletic ability, Jackie left UCLA not only as a hero but a sports legend.

Making collegiate history, Jackie was UCLA's first four-letter man. His outstanding records in basketball, football, track, and baseball led to his induction in the UCLA Sports Hall of Fame in 1984.

ARMY LIFE

He was a true legend. I think more of him as an American citizen who overcame the odds of racial hatred.

—Darryl Strawberry

JACKIE EARNS HIS STRIPES

Jackie was devoted to sports. It gave him an opportunity to display his talents as a way of making his way in the world. His fierce determination could be seen in his steely gaze as he prepared for a game, or in his erect, taut stance on his field of play. When campus bigots hurled racial epithets, he stood his ground. Unbowed by the hardships and buoyed by the triumphs, Jackie exuded confidence. At the beginning of each practice or game, his teammates would hear Jackie's refrain: "We can do it . . . not *if* . . . we can do it."

During his sophomore year at UCLA, the star athlete discovered a new love: Rachel Isum. His teammate and good friend, Ray Bartlett, brought Rachel, a second-year student studying to be a nurse, into the student lounge where Jackie worked part-time. Smitten by her attractive looks and radiant charm, Jackie instantly felt at ease with her and enjoyed talking to her. Although attracted to Jackie, the shy, petite coed was more tentative. She thought that this campus hero with celebrity and confidence had a big head to boot. After several dates, she revised her opinion, discovering that Jackie's hard-charging manner was his way of demonstrating pride in his achievements and the color of his skin. The warmth and understanding of "Rae"—as Jackie called her—had a moderating yet powerful effect on him.

Despite finding love on campus and fame on the field, Jackie decided to leave UCLA after two years. He believed that no matter how many letters he earned or how hard he crammed for exams, a college degree was no guarantee of the type of sports career he was seeking. It was the 1940s, and blacks were not allowed to play in major-league sports, work in major industries alongside whites, or, in the South, use the same public accommodations as whites. Even though Jackie knew Mallie and Rae wanted him to finish college, he desperately wanted to find work to support his family and start building a financial future for himself and the love of his life. After sending out scores of letters for employment in coaching jobs with high schools and colleges, Jackie found his first job in professional sports—sort of.

Everyone thinks of Jackie as a baseball player. But the strapping athlete made his professional sports debut on the gridiron. He spent the fall of 1941 playing football with the Honolulu Bears, a semipro football team. Although it was not a major-league team, it was integrated. He was recruited to the team after they saw how well he played in an exhibition game in which collegiate football stars played the Chicago Bears, the National Football League champions at the time. However, he was given a job working at a construction site during the week and paid one hundred dollars a game playing football on the weekends. His career as a professional football player was cut short, however, when the Japanese bombed Pearl Harbor in Hawaii, and America entered the Second World War. It was time for Robinson to wear yet another uniform: the combat fatigues of the U.S. Army.

Whether running around with the Pepper Street Gang or playing collegiate sports, Jackie was always a leader. But his entry into the Army was a different story. Assigned to ride horseback in the cavalry, the four-letter athlete found that it was much easier to dodge three-hundred-pound men trying to tackle him than to keep from falling off his horse.

Training at the army base at Fort Riley, Kansas, was grueling. Jackie quickly discovered that Jim Crow was not only confined to civilians. The base cafeteria and barracks were segregated so that blacks and whites would have minimal contact. And when Jackie and other black soldiers applied for Officers' Candidate School (OCS), they had to wait to start classes while their white counter-

Jackie's initiative, intelligence, and leadership skills earned him the rank of second lieutenant (far left). But it was no easy feat: Joe Louis (right) used his influence in Washington so that Jackie and other black soldiers could gain admission to Officers' Candidate School.

parts began school, took tests, and assumed their new ranks. Jackie queried his commanding officer about the delays, but his requests were shot down by the brass. Although Jackie could not maneuver the chain of command the way he outran linemen or stole bases, he exhibited the same tenacity that he displayed on the field.

Little did he know that his childhood hero would come to his rescue. One of Jackie's biggest thrills while serving in the Army was the opportunity to meet his hero, heavyweight champion of the world, Joe Louis. Louis was also serving his country in the Army. Jackie was too shy to introduce himself to his childhood idol. A few days after Louis had transferred into Jackie's unit, the boxer walked over and introduced himself. "You're Jackie Robinson. I read a lot about you in the papers. You're quite an athlete, I hear."

Jackie could not believe that the Brown Bomber knew who he was. It would be his most treasured memory of his time in the service. In one of the heart-to-heart conversations between the two, the lean, sinewy All-American shared his frustrations with the broad, bulky prize fighter. Louis, who had put on exhibition bouts to boost the morale of enlisted men at the request of the U.S. War Department, called his contacts in Washington to pressure the Fort Riley Command. Within weeks, Jackie and others were admitted into OCS. Months later, he was wearing the bars of a second lieutenant.

After finally receiving his new rank, Jackie was assigned to a truck battalion of black soldiers and made morale officer. Shortly after his appointment, Jackie's men came to him to complain about conditions in the post exchange, a place on the base where soldiers would gather for snacks and coffee after attending the theater or other activities. Black soldiers were only allowed to sit

R egardless of the ups and downs, Jackie would always receive love and support from his college sweetheart, Rachel.

in a section containing seven seats. Most were forced to stand, even if the many seats designated for white soldiers were unoccupied. After listening to complaint after complaint, Jackie solemnly commented, "I'll try to do something about this."

He could feel that the soldiers didn't believe him. They felt that no black officer had the guts to try to buck the system. Jackie immediately contacted the provost marshal about the lack of seating for blacks. "We are all in this war together," said Jackie, making his appeal by phone. "It seems to me that everyone should have the same basic rights."

The provost marshal dismissed Jackie's requests. Finally, taking for granted that the officer on the other end of the phone was white, the marshal said, "Lieu-

tenant, let me put it this way. How would you like your wife sitting next to a nigger?"

Rage overtook Jackie, and he began shouting at the officer at the top of his lungs. He took the matter to his commanding officer, who had heard the tirade. Jackie wanted to let him know how he was provoked. The commanding officer listened sympathetically and told Jackie that he would write a letter to his superior to change the seating situation and to recommend a reprimand for the provost marshal. Eventually, more seats were allocated for black soldiers, although there were still separate sections for blacks and whites. It may have seemed like a small victory, Jackie thought, but it was a significant one.

Jackie's commanding officer asked him to play football for the base team with the understanding that his skin color would cause him to be banned from certain games. Jackie refused to join the team.

Jackie's refusal resulted in his transfer to Fort Hood, Texas, deep in the heart of the South. The black soldiers dubbed the base "the Hellhole" because of the harsh acts of racism that blacks confronted there. Even though he was an Army officer, he still was not fully accepted, be-

cause of the color of his skin. One time when Jackie was catching the bus on the base to go to a nearby Army hospital to get a checkup, he ran into the wife of one of his fellow lieutenants. Jackie sat in the front of the bus with the woman. The driver glanced into the rearview mirror and saw a black officer talking to a light-complexioned woman that he thought was a white woman. Flustered, the bus driver stopped the bus and ordered Jackie to move to the rear. Jackie would not budge from his seat. He knew his rights: unlike in the civilian South, the Army had issued regulations barring racial discrimination on any vehicle operating on an Army post, a policy that was instituted after such military celebrities as Joe Louis refused to be seated in the back of military buses. At the last stop, the driver told the military police that Jackie was causing trouble.

The incident snowballed, and Jackie was court-martialed. He was put on trial for breaking military rules. He was eventually cleared because of lack of evidence and received an honorable discharge from the Army. However, Jackie decided that he would never wear that uniform again.

Jackie leaves the military. His refusal to sit in the back of the bus led to a court-martial. He was eventually cleared of charges and given an honorable discharge.

A LEAGUE OF THEIR OWN

Jackie Robinson paved the way for African-Americans in baseball. He showed so much heart and poise. Whatever happens to me, I'll never live a day of what he went through in his career.

—Butch Husky

BARNSTORMING WITH THE MONARCHS

When Jackie left the Army, he wondered what he would do next. It was 1944, and he was twenty-five years old with few prospects. To make matters worse, he had to find a way to help support his family as well as earn enough money to marry Rae. He took a job coaching men's basketball at Sam Houston College, a tiny school in Huntsville, Texas, with only thirty-five male students. As coach, Jackie would use his drive and his competitive spirit to lead the school's team to a winning record. In his heart, though, Jackie wanted to be a player.

In those days, a black man, regardless of his ability, was not allowed to play major-league baseball. For black baseball players, the only choice was the Negro leagues. Originally formed in 1920, the Negro leagues had some of the nation's best players: the powerful Josh Gibson, who hit as many as seventy-five homers in one year, was dubbed "The Black Babe Ruth." Satchel Paige could throw so fast that most batters only saw a trail of smoke as they tried to swing at the ball. Cool Papa Bell was known for his daring play and speed in stealing bases. There is no question that players like Gibson, Paige, and Bell would have dominated the majors if they were given a chance to play.

Jackie's opportunity came when he received word that the Kansas City Monarchs were looking for players. At the recommendation of a pitcher who had seen him play in

23

California, Jackie was invited to the Monarchs' Houston training camp. The competition was fierce. Jackie had to go up against Jesse Williams, one of the best players in the Negro league, for starting shortstop. As hard as he tried, Robinson was unable to unseat the veteran. Jackie owes his start in professional baseball in part to just plain luck: Williams injured his arm, and Jackie got the spot. He would have to practice hard between games and increase his speed to keep the position.

For Jackie and the other Negro leaguers, playing professional baseball meant long hours on the road and little chance to see their families. Jackie longed to be with Rae, who was back in California. He began to sense in her letters that her patience was wearing thin.

The Negro league teams played as many as four games a day and traveled long hours in old buses that broke down frequently. In those days, life on the road was called barnstorming. It was not unusual for Jackie and his teammates to leave Kansas City on Sunday night, arrive in Philadelphia on Tuesday morning, play a double-header that night, and then hit the road again after finishing the games. The pace was grueling. Furthermore, the

Jackie met some of baseball's finest when he played with the Kansas City Monarchs (far left) in the Negro leagues. Despite constant travel, Jim Crow laws, and no prospect of going to the majors, the Negro leaguers always dazzled fans with spectacular play.

Negro leaguers ate and slept in their buses since restaurants or hotels would rarely let them in.

Dealing with racism on a daily basis, most players followed the rules of Jim Crow. The proud Jackie tried to find ways to chip away at the system. Once when the team stopped at a gas station in Oklahoma, Jackie turned the tables on the owner. The team had been stopping at the one-room gas station for thirty years, and the owner would pump gas into the bus's two fifty-gallon tanks. "I'm going to the rest room," Jackie demanded. "Boy, you can't go to that rest room," the owner challenged. Knowing the owner could not normally sell one hundred gallons of gas in a whole year, Jackie told him to "take the hose out of the tank. If we can't use the rest room, we will not pay for gas here. We'll get it someplace else." The owner caved in. "Well, you boys can go to the rest room, but don't stay long." Whether in Pasadena, the military, or a roadside gas station, Jackie always took the opportunity to clip the wings of Jim Crow.

The thing that kept the Negro leaguers going was the love of the game. For Jackie, it was also the chance to perfect his game, learning from some of the best players in the league. For example, when Jackie joined the Monarchs in 1945, he got a chance to play with the legendary Satchel Paige, a lanky, outgoing showman with a huge arsenal of pitches to strike out ballplayers. Paige was such a great player that St. Louis Cardinal pitching legend Dizzy Dean said, "My fastball looks like a change of pace alongside that little pistol bullet ol' Satch shoots up the plate."

The legendary Satchel Paige winds up to throw one of his lightning-fast pitches. Pitching great Dizzy Dean considered him the best pitcher in organized ball.

Jackie, who played the shortstop position, was amazed by some of Paige's antics and the yarns spun about him. During one game against the Monarchs' major rivals, the Homestead Grays, Paige called in the outfield as he proceeded to pitch to the league's most powerful batter, the huge, hulking Josh Gibson. Slowly, Paige walked around the mound, wound up, and whipped the ball across the plate.

With every pitch he threw, the crowd would gasp as the great Gibson swung. Before he threw the last pitch, Satchel boasted, "I'm not gonna throw any smoke around your yoke. I'm gonna throw a pea around your knee." Looking at the ball speeding by him, the great Josh Gibson struck out.

Jackie watched the great players and learned from their example. He took mental notes of Gibson's hitting style and the base-stealing prowess of Cool Papa Bell of the Pittsburgh Crawfords, who was considered the fastest man on the baseball diamond. Jackie learned, among other things, how to navigate the base paths and the fine art of stealing home plate. His hard work and study would pay off again and again. During that season, Robinson led the Monarchs in hitting, belting ten doubles, four triples, and five homers.

Clockwise from photo at upper left: Cool Papa Bell, considered the fastest man in baseball, demonstrates his prowess on the field; Josh Gibson, "The Black Babe Ruth," takes home plate; Jesse Williams, the man Jackie Robinson had to compete with for his slot on the Monarchs; and Buck O'Neil looks out at the action from the Monarchs' dugout.

JACKIE'S DREAM

Jackie worked hard for each and every one of us

—Ken Griffey Jr.

BREAKING THE COLOR BARRIER

As Jackie was making a reputation for himself as a sensation in the Negro leagues, he dreamed of breaking the color line in major-league sports. Jackie had always believed that the demonstration of excellence would show that blacks were qualified to take advantage of opportunities in American society. That is why he worked so hard to become a skilled athlete in college and a hard-driving leader in the Army.

He also knew the disappointment of being overlooked. In 1945, Wendell Smith, a sportswriter for the *Pittsburgh Courier,* then the nation's largest black newspaper, used his influence to get Jackie and two other Negro league stars a tryout with the Boston Red Sox. For years, black sportswriters such as Smith and Sam Lacy of the *Baltimore Afro-American* had been trying to pressure major-league baseball to recruit from this untapped wellspring of talent. But like this mock tryout, their efforts produced no immediate results.

Back east in New York City, someone else was also thinking about integration. Branch Rickey, the president of the Brooklyn Dodgers, decided that it was time to hire from this bumper crop of stellar athletes. The choice was extremely personal for Rickey. He remembered that in 1910 when he was a college coach at Ohio Wesleyan, he could not register one of the members of his team—a black man—at hotels when they were on the road. The indignity that the player suffered stuck with Rickey for more than forty years.

In 1945, Jackie ushers in a new era of baseball by signing with the Brooklyn Dodgers to become the first African-American to play major-league baseball this century. The historic action by Jackie and the Brooklyn Dodgers' president, Branch Rickey, paved the way for integration in professional sports—and other aspects of American life.

"Rickey needed a player with a college education and the courage to bear verbal—maybe even physical—abuse without striking back. He believed that Jackie was his man."

Rickey started sending scouts to Negro league games, telling the press he was recruiting an all-black team to play when the Dodgers were away. The reports came back about a number of top-notch black ballplayers—Paige, Gibson, and Bell among them—but the one who stood out to the cigar-chomping Rickey was the hard-hitting, swift-running shortstop for the Kansas City Monarchs—Jackie Robinson.

Rickey needed a player with a college education and the courage to bear verbal—maybe even physical—abuse without striking back. He believed that Jackie was his man.

On the hottest summer day in August 1945, Jackie and the Dodgers' scout, Clyde Sukeforth, went to the team's headquarters in Brooklyn. Jackie recalled the conversation he had had earlier with Clyde. "Branch Rickey is interested in you. He wants to meet you in New York," Clyde had told him. Jackie had just shrugged. Negro league players did not expect much from the major leagues. But now that he was riding up to the fourth floor to meet one of the most revered men in baseball, Jackie started to sweat. And it was not because of the weather.

After some small talk, the imposing Rickey said in his deep, booming voice, "I am interested in you as a candidate for the Brooklyn Dodgers of the National League. I think you can play in the majors. What do you think?"

Jackie was stunned. He could not utter a word. Rickey continued, "You think you could play for Montreal, our minor-league team?"

"Yes," Jackie said simply.

After making Jackie the offer, Rickey asked, "Have you the guts to play, no matter what?"

Jackie answered, "I can play the game, Mr. Rickey."

Rickey explained, "Well, this is what's going to happen. White people all over America are going to see a black man play against, and even more importantly, *with* white men. Many of them are not going to like it. You are going to get letters filled with hate and fear. Some may even threaten you."

At long last, Jackie married his true love, Rachel, at the Independent Church in Los Angeles. Presiding over the nuptials was Pastor Karl Downs, Jackie's first mentor.

"Mr. Rickey, do you want a ballplayer who is afraid to fight back?" Jackie asked.

"Mr. Robinson, I'm looking for a ballplayer with the guts enough *not* to fight back. Because the only way for a black man to break the color line is not to retaliate." Then Rickey whispered, "Three years, Mr. Robinson. Three years. That's what I'm asking you. At the end of those three years, I give you my word you can say and do what you want. Because, if you do what I say, there will be more and more black players in baseball."

Jackie looked into Branch Rickey's eyes. "Mr. Rickey, I've got to do it." The two shook hands. It was a handshake that would change baseball—and America.

BREAKING THE COLOR LINE

Before he could suit up in an official Dodgers uniform, Jackie first had to prove himself in the minor leagues. Minor-league "farm clubs" are where new professional players improve their skills until they are ready for the big leagues. Jackie was slated to play for the Montreal Royals, the top farm team for the Dodgers.

Spring training with the Royals was rough for Jackie and Rae, whom he married after he signed with the team. They had to go south to Daytona Beach, Florida, where the team prepared for the season. As they left to go to the airport to catch their flight, Mallie gave Jackie

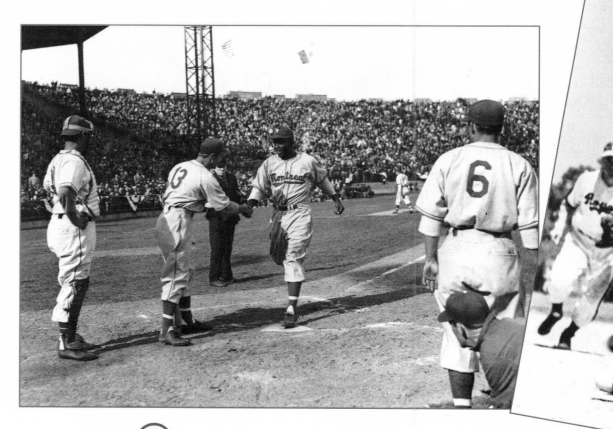

J ackie started his major-league career in the minors. Playing for the Montreal Royals, the Brooklyn Dodgers' farm team, Jackie distinguished himself as the International League's Most Valuable Player in 1946.

and Rae a shoebox of fried chicken. Even though they were embarrassed by the stereotype that Mallie's offering conjured up, they took it as they departed.

Their troubles started when their plane arrived in New Orleans. The Robinsons were not allowed to get on their connecting flight or to eat in the cafeteria. The only meal available to them was Mallie's chicken. When the Robinsons reached Pensacola, Florida, the next day, Jackie and his wife were forced to sit in the back of the bus. Rae quietly cried as Jackie pledged not to fight back.

Jackie was not greeted by the welcome wagon when he arrived in Florida. His teammates avoided him. The team was not permitted to play in an exhibition game in Sanford, Florida, because it was against the law for whites and blacks to play together. But Jackie had endured tough trials and he thought he could get through this one. His first game was in Jersey City. As the Montreal Royals got set to play the Jersey City Giants, Jackie took his position as a second baseman. The sun shone brightly on spacious Roosevelt Stadium as band music played and the fresh smell of hot dogs and peanuts filled the air. The 25,000–seat stadium was choked with more

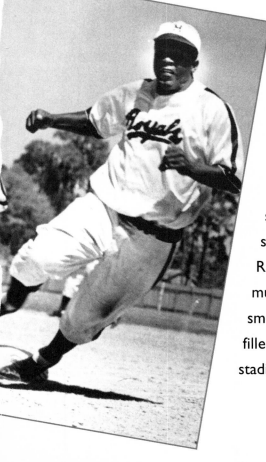

On April 10, 1947, Jackie hung up his Montreal Royals uniform and emerged from the team locker room as a Dodger.

than 51,000 people. Thousands of black fans came out to root for Jackie. In the top of the third inning, the Giants' pitcher tried to sneak a fastball by him. Jackie drove the ball over 340 feet for his first home run. The crowd exploded in cheers, even though he was playing for the opposing team. He smiled as he saw Rae in the stands. But his grin grew even broader as his teammates came to congratulate him and welcome him to the team. Later in the game, Jackie stole two bases. Beaming Branch Rickey said of Jackie's first game: "That's a pretty good way to break into organized baseball."

Jackie takes time out to play with his son, little Jackie.

Led by Jackie, Montreal won the International League pennant in the Junior World Series that season. It was not an easy season for Robinson, who faced racial taunts from opponents, baseball fans, and even his own team. Jackie wanted to confront his tormentors but remembered his promise to Branch Rickey. He met his detractors with grace and dignity. Performance overcame prejudice, and Jackie was named Most Valuable Player in the league. The bigger reward for Jackie was being mobbed and cheered by the fans who didn't seem to care that he was a black man, but just a great ballplayer.

On April 9, 1947, the Dodgers issued a press release announcing that they had signed Jackie Robinson to suit up as a major-league player. As in the past, Jackie had to prove himself all over again.

Breaking the color line and entering the majors was no easy feat. Jackie's signing was announced two years before the military was integrated, eight years before school desegregation, and a decade before the start of the Civil Rights movement. Jackie's face had been plastered in all of the newspapers as the first African-American to play major-league baseball this century. Reactions to his signing to play for the Dodgers were mixed. Many questioned his ability to play. Wearing his neatly pressed blue-and-gray wool uniform—number 42—Jackie took on a heavy burden, knowing that he had to succeed.

Jackie did not receive a warm reception from all of his teammates. Shortly after Jackie joined the Dodgers, his teammate Eddie Stanky walked up to him.

"I want you to know something," Stanky said, pointing his finger at Jackie. "You're on this ball club and as far as I'm concerned that makes you one of twenty-five players on my team. But before I play with you I want you to know I don't like it. I want you to know I don't like you."

Jackie stared right back into Stanky's eyes and replied in a calm, steady voice, "All right. That's the way I'd rather have it. Right out in the open."

Jackie earned the respect and comradeship of his teammates Johnny "Spider" Jorgensen, Pee Wee Reese, and Ed Stanky.

Other team members—many of whom came from the South and had never interacted with African-Americans as equals—circulated a petition protesting Jackie's new slot on the Dodger team as a first baseman. Rickey uncovered the ringleaders and scolded them individually, asserting that anyone who was not willing to have a black teammate could quit.

The cold shoulder he received from his team was nothing compared to the abuse he received from oppo-

nents and spectators. Pitchers threw lightning-quick pitches at his body when he stood at the plate. Players would slide into Jackie's base with the spiked heels of their cleats aimed high. On the field, he withstood jeers, boos, and insults, and in the locker room, he received threatening letters. With hostility from his opponents and little support from his teammates, Jackie got off to a poor start in the major leagues. In his first four games, he went to bat twenty times without a base hit. Many were saying that Jackie was not ready for the big leagues. Discouraged, Jackie thought the same thing. Burt Shotten, the Dodgers' manager, called him aside. "Jackie, you're putting too much pressure on yourself. I won't take you out of the lineup. Relax and the hits will fall."

Jackie's next game was against the Phillies. The Phillies' dugout hurled insults at him every time he came up to bat. Ben Chapman, the Phillies' big, tobacco-spewing manager, told his players that "there was a $5,000 fine for anyone who didn't go after Robinson." And they did just that. He could hear the jeers from the Phillies' dugout. "Nigger, go back to the cotton fields," cried one. "Go back to the bushes," yelled another. When Jackie went out to bat, the Phillies sent a black cat out to home plate.

Jackie was starting to crack. How long can I remain patient? he asked himself. Then Jackie decided to strike back—on the field. Jackie hit a single. He also stole three bases, including home plate, winning the game for the Dodgers. When Jackie received further verbal abuse from the Phillies, he discovered that he had a surprising new defender: his teammate Eddie Stanky. "Why don't you yell at somebody who can answer back?" Stanky shouted at the Phillies in defense of his teammate.

Jackie's stellar play earned him the respect, admiration, and friendship of his teammates. Jackie was a power hitter, batting .297 and knocking twelve home runs out of the park his first year. He ranked second in the league in runs scored. And he could run: Jackie bunted for nineteen hits and led the league with twenty-nine stolen bases. His efforts helped the Dodgers beat the St. Louis Cardinals to win the 1947 National League pennant. Many of the naysayers who thought Jackie would not last

his first season voted for him to be Rookie of the Year. At the end of the season, more than 26,000 fans crowded into Ebbets Field to salute Jackie. Throughout the season, new attendance records were set in Brooklyn, Philadelphia, Pittsburgh, Cincinnati, and Chicago. Wendell Smith wrote: "Jackie's nimble / Jackie's quick / Jackie's making the turnstiles click." Jackie's detractors were starting to turn around. In fact, by the end of the season, Phillies' manager Ben Chapman said, "Robinson is a major leaguer in every respect."

Although the Dodgers did not win the World Series that year, Jackie realized a greater victory—two other black ballplayers signed major-league contracts. Dan Bankhead joined the Dodgers, and the Cleveland Indians signed up Larry Doby, the first black to play in the American League. In fact, Jackie paved the way for pitching legend Satchel Paige. The old barnstormer finally made it to the majors with the Cleveland Indians and, in 1948 at the ripe age of forty-two, became the oldest rookie ever to play professional baseball. Jackie's dream that the major leagues would be fully integrated seemed like it might finally come true.

Stealing 197 bases in his career, Jackie was one of the few players bold enough to capture home plate.

OFF TO THE WORLD SERIES

Jackie Robinson accomplished more than winning awards and pennants and a World Series. With poise and grace and steely determination he pushed open a door that should never have been closed, and held it open for the countless talented young men and women who would follow him. America is a stronger nation because of Jackie Robinson.

—President Bill Clinton

JACKIE ROBINSON, SUPERSTAR

I t was dubbed the Golden Era of the Brooklyn Dodgers. Of the sixteen teams that made up the major leagues, the Dodgers was the dream team of the Radio Age. By 1948, Jackie was moved from first base to second base, where he worked side by side with Pee Wee Reese, the team's captain, who played shortstop. Fans crowded the stadium to watch the duo—"the heart and soul of the Brooklyn Dodgers"—make double plays. It was an opportunity for the fans to witness not only great plays on the field but a black man and a white man playing together.

After three years of play, Jackie responded to racist actions and Jim Crow. For example, in St. Louis, he protested that he and other black players were not able to stay in the Chase Hotel with their white teammates. If we are all team members, Jackie reasoned, then all should be treated equally. To avoid the adverse publicity, the Chase Hotel gave in to Jackie's demands. These were stands that Jackie made before the Civil Rights movement became a full-scale campaign in the mid-1950s. For African-Americans, who jammed into ballparks or huddled around radios when he played, Jackie was a source of pride: a black man who could prove himself on the playing field and was not afraid to speak his mind when the cheering stopped. And off the playing field, he was a loving husband and father.

Even though he still confronted racism, Jackie had become America's first black superstar. Over the years, his graceful slides into home plate and his amazing catches were examples of

Jackie slides into home plate as catcher Yogi Berra tries to tag him. It looks too close to call. ▼

In the eighth inning, Umpire Summers signals that Jackie is safe while batter Frank Kellart and the Yankees' awestruck catcher Yogi Berra look on. Berra takes off his catcher's mask as he argues with the ump over his call. However, Summers's resolve remains unshaken. He gestures that Jackie scored. It will not be the last time that Jackie frustrates Berra during the 1955 World Series. ▶

Bottom of the third inning, Jackie tags Yankee catcher Yogi Berra at third base after fielding a ground ball from the Yankees' batter Bob Cerv. He whips the ball to first base to get out Cerv. It's unbelievable—the Dodgers make their 11th double play, a record for a team in the World Series. ▼

his athletic excellence. Jackie hit a grand slam homer that earned the Dodgers another pennant in 1949. He became that year's Most Valuable Player in the National League. In 1952 and 1953 the Dodgers won the pennant again, largely because of Jackie's fielding, homers, and stolen bases. In 1953, he drove in 95 runs, scored 109 runs, and stole 17 bases.

"Jackie became 1949's Most Valuable Player in the National League. In 1952 and 1953 the Dodgers won the pennant again, largely because of Jackie's fielding, homers, and stolen bases. In 1953, he drove in 95 runs, scored 109 runs, and stole 17 bases."

As his star shone brightly, Jackie's salary grew from his starting wage of $5,000 a year to $35,000 a year—in an age before superstars earned million-dollar paychecks. He was the first black man to appear on the cover of *Life* magazine and to endorse products, ranging from cigarettes to candy bars. During those years, what eluded Jackie and the Dodgers was a victory in the World Series. They were always defeated by their crosstown rivals, the mighty New York Yankees. "Wait till next year" was the rallying cry of the Dodgers and their fans.

In 1955, the Dodgers would once again face the Yankees in the World Series. Jackie, who was now thirty-six, was older, heavier, and slower, but he still had his spirit. The Yankees took the lead in the opening game. In the eighth inning, with the Dodgers trailing, Jackie had made it to third base. Feeling as if he had his old magic, Jackie danced off the base, just as he had done since he was a child playing in the sandlot.

Whitey Ford, who was pitching for the Yankees, ignored Jackie. He believed that Jackie was no longer the base-stealing threat he had once been. But on Ford's second pitch to the plate, Jackie took off. With his lightning-quick glide, he ran to home plate and made an incredible hook slide, just beating the catcher's tag. Jackie stole home plate.

It was the type of play and energy that won the Dodgers the World Series that year. Jackie finally got his championship ring. The 1955 World Series was the highlight of his career. Two years later, Jackie would hang up his cleats—for good.

Surrounded by Branch Rickey, Rachel Robinson, and his mother, Mallie, Jackie savors one of baseball's highest honors—induction into the Baseball Hall of Fame in Cooperstown, NY.

Jackie felt his greatest achievement was not the 1955 World Series but helping get more African-American ballplayers in the game. Citing Jackie's example, most of the National and American League teams started recruiting African-Americans to play against—and alongside—whites.

The crowning moment of his baseball career was on July 23, 1962. In his first year of eligibility, Jackie was voted by baseball writers to the National Baseball Hall of Fame in Cooperstown, NY. The crowd of 5,000 watched as the first black man to play in the major leagues was officially acknowledged as one of the all-time great ballplayers. Fittingly, three people joined Jackie on the podium as he received the award: Mallie, Rachel, and Branch Rickey. Jackie told the crowd that it was an honor he would never forget.

After baseball, Jackie continued to be a strong voice, joining the Civil Rights movement and pushing black participation in the corporate world. He remained true to his oft-said maxim: "A life is not important, except in the impact it has on other lives."

April 15, 1997—Major-league baseball, along with Rachel Robinson and President Bill Clinton, applauded Jackie Robinson's contribution to the sport and the nation by retiring his uniform—number 42—in perpetuity.

The photo above shows Jackie on the day he retired from baseball.

On October 24, 1972, Jackie Robinson died after battling his last foe—diabetes.

The accomplishments and spirit of the man were honored on April 15, 1997—the fiftieth anniversary of his first major-league game. At the ceremony, which was attended by Rachel Robinson and President Bill Clinton, Jackie's uniform, number 42, was retired for perpetuity among all major-league teams because Jackie "was and remains bigger than the game."

Jackie Robinson helped make it possible for every-

one to make it to the major leagues—not just in baseball, but in every aspect of life. Without Jackie Robinson, there would have been no Hank Aaron, no Ken Griffey Jr., no Tiger Woods, nor even Michael Jordan. He proved to the world that ability is what matters, not the color of your skin. Whenever we see ballplayers of different races playing together, or kids of different colors choosing up sides for a sandlot game, we owe it to him.

Jackie Robinson's spirit lives on.

1619
Twenty black indentured servants, the first African-Americans in the North American English colonies, arrive in Jamestown, Virginia.

1845
The New York Knickerbocker Club, which set the rules for baseball, is organized. They allow free blacks and integrated teams to play.

1857
National Association of Baseball Players is organized.

The Dred Scott Decision by the U.S. Supreme Court denies citizenship to African-Americans, whether they are free or slaves.

1860
Slave states in the South secede from the Union and form a separate national government. This action leads to the Civil War.

1862
During the Civil War, Congress authorizes the recruitment of blacks for military service. African-American soldiers learn the fundamentals of baseball and play on integrated teams.

1865
The Thirteenth Amendment, officially abolishing slavery in the United States, is ratified.

1867
The Brooklyn Uniques and the Philadelphia Excelsiors play in the first "Negro Baseball Championship."

1868
The Fourteenth Amendment, guaranteeing African-Americans citizenship, becomes a part of the U.S. Constitution.

1869
The Philadelphia Pythians become the first all-black baseball team to compete against an all-white squad, the City Items.

1870
The Fifteenth Amendment becomes a part of the U.S. Constitution, declaring that no citizen can be denied the right to vote because of race.

1871
The National Association of Professional Baseball Players is organized. The Philadelphia Pythians are denied membership.

1872
African-American baseball player John "Bud" Fowler plays for a local white team in Newcastle, Pa.

1875
Riding the race horse Aristides, African-American jockey Oliver Lewis wins the first Kentucky Derby ever held.

The Civil Rights Bill is enacted by Congress, giving African-Americans the right to equal treatment in public places and transportation.

1876
The National Baseball League is founded.

1877
Reconstruction ends in the South and state governments enact severe laws to regulate African-Americans.

1881
Tennessee passes the first "Jim Crow" law, requiring railroad companies to provide segregated cars for African-Americans. Similar laws are adopted by all southern states.

1883
The 1875 Civil Rights Act is declared invalid by the U.S. Supreme Court.

1884
Moses Fleetwood Walker becomes starting catcher for the Toledo Mudhens, a minor-league team.

1885
The Cuban Giants, considered the first black professional baseball team, is formed.

1896
The U.S. Supreme Court upholds "separate but equal" railroad accommodations in the *Plessy v. Ferguson* case.

Bert Jones is forced out of the Kansas State Baseball League. He is believed to be the last African-American to play on an integrated team until Jackie Robinson breaks the color barrier in 1947.

1898
Many blacks lose the right to vote when literacy tests and poll taxes are upheld by the U.S. Supreme Court.

Marshall "Major" Taylor is declared national cycling champion. The League of American Wheelmen, however, refuses to recognize his status and chooses a white champion.

1908
Jack Johnson knocks out Tommy Burns, becoming the first African-American to hold the world heavyweight boxing title.

John Baxter Taylor becomes the first African-American to win an Olympic gold medal by winning the 4x400-meter medley in London.

1909
The National Association for the Advancement of Colored People (NAACP) is founded. The NAACP pushes for integration of the Olympics.

1911
Pitcher Andrew "Rube" Foster, who became known as the "Father of Black Baseball," forms the Chicago American Giants.

The National Urban League is founded to assist southern blacks migrating to the North. The Urban League joins the NAACP in its fight to integrate the Olympics.

1914
Joseph Louis Barrow, the "Brown Bomber," is born. As Joe Louis, the boxer will hold a record of 68 wins, with 54 knockouts.

1916
Fritz Pollard, running back for Brown University, becomes the first African-American to play in the Rose Bowl.

1919
Fritz Pollard joins the Akron (Ohio) Indians to become the first black professional football player.

Jackie Robinson is born.

1920
Rube Foster organizes the National Negro Baseball League.

1921
The National Football Association is organized.

The Harlem Renaissance, a period in which blacks make outstanding contributions to the arts, begins.

1923
The New York Rens become the first black professional basketball team.

1924
The first Negro League World Series is held.

1926
Boxer Theodore Flowers wins the world middleweight championship.

1932
The New York Rens win the world basketball championship by beating the Boston Celtics.

1936
Jesse Owens wins four gold medals in track events at the Berlin Olympics.

1937
Joe Louis defeats James Braddock, becoming the heavyweight boxing champion of the world.

1941
The United States enters World War II. The War Department announces the formation of the first Army Air Corps squadron for black cadets.

1945
World War II ends.

Jackie Robinson signs with the Kansas City Monarchs. In October, Robinson makes history when he signs with the Brooklyn Dodgers.

1946
The Los Angeles Rams sign Kenny Washington and Woody Strode, who become the first blacks to join contemporary pro football. The Cleveland Browns of the All-American Football Conference sign Bill Willis and Marion Motley.

1947
Jackie Robinson becomes the first African-American to play for a major-league baseball club.

1948
In the London Olympics, Alice Coachman wins a gold medal for the high jump, becoming the first black woman to win a gold medal.

1958
Willie O'Ree, playing for the Boston Bruins, is the first African-American in the National Hockey League.

1960
The Negro American League disbands.

1962
Wilt Chamberlain of the Philadelphia 76ers scores 100 points in a single game against the New York Knicks, a score which he would achieve again but would never be matched by any other basketball player in history.

Jackie Robinson is inducted into the National Baseball Hall of Fame.

1963

Basketball superstar Michael Jordan is born.

Over 250,000 participate in the March on Washington at the Lincoln Memorial, one of the largest protest assemblies in U.S. history. Martin Luther King Jr. delivers his "I Have a Dream" speech.

1964

Cassius Clay knocks out Sonny Liston to become heavyweight champion of the world. Later the same year, he changes his name to Muhammad Ali to reflect his religious conversion.

Congress passes the Civil Rights Bill, banning discrimination in public accommodations, education, and employment.

1965

Leroy "Satchel" Paige is named all-time outstanding player by the National Baseball Congress.

1966

Emmett Ashford becomes the first African-American umpire in baseball's major leagues.

Bill Russell, a basketball star with the Boston Celtics, joins the team's coaching staff to become the first African-American to coach a major athletic team.

1968

Arthur Ashe is the first African-American to win the U.S. Open men's singles tennis championship.

1970

Bodybuilder Chris Dickerson is the first black Mr. America.

1971

Satchel Paige is inducted into the Baseball Hall of Fame.

1972

Jackie Robinson dies.

1974

Hank Aaron hits his 715th home run, breaking Babe Ruth's major-league record.

Professional golfer Lee Elder wins the Monsanto Open in Pensacola, Florida, becoming the first African-American to qualify for the Masters Tournament.

Frank Robinson becomes manager of the Cleveland Indians, the first African-American manager in the major leagues.

1975

Arthur Ashe becomes the first black man to win the men's singles tennis title at Wimbledon.

1980

William Davenport and Jeff Gadley, part of a four-man bobsled team, are the first African-Americans to compete in the Winter Olympics.

1983

Jesse Jackson launches a bid to become the Democratic nominee for President.

1985

Eddie Robinson, football coach of Grambling State University, becomes the longest-winning football coach in history.

1988

Debi Thomas wins the bronze medal in figure skating, becoming the first African-American to win a medal in the Winter Olympics.

Mae C. Jemison is the first African-American to become a U.S. astronaut.

1989

Bill White, former first baseman for the St. Louis Cardinals, the Philadelphia Phillies, and the New York and San Francisco Giants, is chosen president of the National Baseball League, the first African-American ever to hold a top executive position in a major U.S. professional sports league.

1992

Michael Jordan earns his sixth straight National Basketball League scoring title, cited as "the most exciting player ever to play pro basketball."

1993

After helping the Chicago Bulls win three championships in a row, Michael Jordan retires from basketball.

Mannie Jackson becomes the first African-American owner of the Harlem Globetrotters.

Arthur Ashe dies.

1995

Michael Jordan returns to basketball. The stock market realizes an additional $2 billion in value based on his announcement.

1996

Bob Watson, general manager for the New York Yankees, becomes the first black general manager to win the World Series.

1997

Tiger Woods becomes the first African-American—and youngest golfer—to win the Masters Tournament.

ACKNOWLEDGMENTS

The ambitious task of chronicling the life of Jackie Robinson could not have been achieved without the assistance and support of a number of outstanding people. I would like to thank Dwayne McDuffie, my business partner and the editor-in-chief of Milestone Media, whose professional insight and editorial instincts proved invaluable to producing this book, and Pamela Johnson, whose creative input was essential in shaping this material.

I thank also Deidra Varona of Major League Baseball Properties for her direction and resources on the Negro leagues; John Skipper and Beverly Cole, who provided much support; Charles Frazier for his artistic talent and intimate knowledge of baseball history; Roy Johnson for reviewing the manuscript and lending his expertise; Stacey Robinson for research help; the staffs of the Schomburg Center for Social Research; the Baseball Hall of Fame; and the Smithsonian Institute.

Finally, I am grateful to my editor, Katherine Tegen, and her team, designer Stephanie Bart-Horvath, and photo researcher Zoe Moffitt for their dedication, energy, and patience on this fulfilling project.

SELECTED BIBLIOGRAPHY

Books

Asante, Molefi K., and Mark T. Mattson. *The Historical and Cultural Atlas of African Americans.* New York: Macmillan, 1991.

Ashe, Arthur. *Hard Road To Glory,* vols. I, II, and III. New York: Amistad, 1993.

Dixon, Phil, and Patrick J. Hannigan. *The Negro Baseball Leagues: A Photographic History.* Mattituck, NY: Amereon House, 1992.

Faulkner, David. *Great Time Coming: The Life of Jackie Robinson.* New York: Simon and Schuster, 1995.

Kahn, Roger. *The Boys of Summer.* New York: Harper and Row, 1972.

McKissack, Patricia, and Frederick McKissack Jr. *Black Diamond: Story of the Negro Leagues.* New York: Scholastic, 1994.

Robinson, Jackie, with Alfred Duckett. *I Never Had It Made: An Autobiography.* New York: Putnam, 1972.

Robinson, Rachel, with Lee Daniels. *Jackie Robinson: An Intimate Portrait.* New York: Abrams, 1996.

Trouppe, Quincy, *20 Years Too Soon.* New York: S&S Enterprises, 1972.

Tygiel, Jules, ed. *Baseball's Great Experiment: Jackie Robinson and His Legacy.* New York: Oxford University Press, 1983.

Tygiel, Jules, ed. *The Jackie Robinson Reader.* New York: The Penguin Group, 1997.

Ward, Geoffrey, and Ken Burns. *Baseball: An Illustrated History.* New York: Knopf, 1994.

Film & Newsreels

The Brooklyn Dodgers: America's Baseball Team.

History of the Black American Athlete

Jackie Robinson: Barrier Breaker (Smithsonian Associate Seminar)

The Jackie Robinson Story

Twilight at Noon: The Jackie Robinson Story

When It Was a Game

Articles

"Aaron Hopes Robinson's Legacy Won't Be Forgotten," *Associated Press,* 15 April 1997.

"Baseball Salutes Robinson," *USA Today,* 16 April 1997.

"Jackie's Legacy Lives with Locals," *New York Post,* 15 April 1997.

"Robinson Changed Minds and Won Hearts," *Chicago Tribune,* 31 March 1997.

PHOTO CREDITS